Awakening Your Chakras

Seven Jewels of Magical Transformation

by Jewels

Jewels of Light Publishing
14300 NE 20th Avenue D-102 #383
Vancouver, WA 98686
1.855.50 JEWEL (505.3935)
JewelsofLight.com

Copyright 2013 - Jewels of Light, LLC
All rights reserved.

Cover & Interior Design by: Dianne Leonetti - DzinerGraphics.com
Chakra drawings by Karen Foster Wells

ISBN: 978-1893037-07-6

Jewels of Light Publishing ©2013

Awakening Your Chakras

> IMPORTANT: This book is not intended to substitute for the advice of physicians or other health care providers. It offers information to help the reader cooperate with health professionals in a joint approach to the achievement of optimal health.

All rights reserved. Neither this book nor any part may be reproduced or transmitted in any form or by any means, electronic or mechanical, including photocopying, microfilming and recording, or by any information storage and retrieval system, without permission in writing from the publisher.

This book is dedicated to the Jewels of my life

My lovely daughters

Alyssa and Arielle

Our Soul's Journey

The disciple said to Jesus, *"Speak to us about our end: How will it look? How will it happen?* Jesus replied, *"Have you found the beginning in yourselves? If not, why are you asking about the end? For in the place in yourselves where you find the beginning, you will also find the end. The Blessed ones will find their feet standing at the beginning. They will know the end and will not taste death."*
– Gospel of Thomas

As a being destined to remember who you are, you have been gifted with a physical body as a vehicle for this journey. Your outer life will manifest many stories, many relationships, many changes, and you will most likely sometimes experience pain and suffering, while other times peace and happiness.

Life has a secret that is available to you and that secret holds the immense wisdom of your life. Remembering back when you were a child and the things you did growing up, there was always something that witnessed your life. Throughout your adult life the witness continues to see and sometimes this witness offers you guidance and wisdom on your path.

Who is this witness?
When asking deeply, you can freely and simply see it is your own true consciousness which is awareness itself. When attention is turned back toward this awareness you discover that you are on an eternal journey of expansion beyond the temporary expressions of this one life.

Introduction *5*

The Seven Jewels of Magical Transformation *6*

The Wish Fulfilling Tree *7*

The Auras and Energy Fields *8*

The Kundalini Life Force *10*

The Seven Major Chakras *12*

Your Higher Self Meditation *26*

The Heart Initiation *27*

The Three Higher Chakras
Soul Star *28* – Soul Purpose *30* – Destiny *32*

The Art of Meditation *34*

Journey Through the Chakras: Color Meditation *36*
Color Healing the Aura and Chakras *37*

Clearing the Chakras Through Your Healing Hands *38*
Daily Chakra Clearing Meditation
Meditation and Gemstones

Chakra Kinesiology Test *39*
Energy Evaluation Using the Pendulum

Breathing Deeply & Chakra Sounds *40*

Angelic Chakra Meditation *41*

Chakras in Relationship to Your Health *42*

Aromatherapy Through Chakra Fragrances *43*
Balancing Chakras Through Nature

Essential Oils: Nature's Fragrant Garden *44*
How to use Essential Oils
The Bach Flowers for the Chakras

Symptoms – Essential Oils For: *45*

The Healing Power of Crystals & Gemstones *46*

Gems & Balancing the Seven Primary Chakras *47*

Daily Chakra Balancing Exercises *48*

About Jewels & Jewels of Light Products *51*

Introduction

The Seven Chakras are the *Jewels of Light* located along the spinal cord. It is important to keep them clear and balanced, allowing a free flow of energy through the spine so that your Spirit is free to express the radiant being that you are, unencumbered by accumulated or unresolved issues.

Balancing the chakras can be accomplished through guided meditations, yoga and movement, energy healing methods and connecting with nature. When your chakras are balanced you will have a greater vitality and increased sense of joy and well-being. Since the chakras are deeply interconnected with energy fields and our connection to Spirit, by keeping them balanced you will achieve vibrant well-being.

This book will provide you with information on the seven major chakras as well as the three higher chakras. In this book you'll find many ways to connect with your chakras and your energy. You can use any or all of the methods here to help keep your chakras balanced and assist in transforming your life so you may live to your fullest potential. Listen to your body and intuition and enjoy this magical journey of transformation through your chakras.

*"Wisdom is knowing I am nothing,
Love is knowing I am everything,
and between the two my life moves."*
– Nisargadatta Maharaj

The Seven Jewels of Magical Transformation

Looking at the wonder of nature, we can see magic everywhere. Magic is the life force that animates all of nature, and nature is what we truly are. *Awakening Your Chakras* is a path to becoming your best self, and reaching for your highest potential.

The 1st Jewel of Awakening originates from your Ground of Being related to the **Root Chakra.** When this Jewel is shining brightly there is a feeling of oneness with life, and all of nature. You begin your journey of transformation from this ground of your being by affirming your sacred contract and saying "Yes" to your life purpose.

The 2nd Jewel of Awakening is the gift of Energy and Confidence – the **Navel Chakra.** The creative energy that is within you is the same energy that has created the most awe-inspiring expressions of nature. The universal blueprint of this center is expressed as confidence and creativity. It is a vessel for the life force of pure potential.

The 3rd Jewel of Awakening is founded in Courage and Strength related to the **Solar Plexus Chakra.** You are on a path of awakening, a path that is guiding you to discover what is true beyond your conditioning and known identification. It takes courage and inner strength to make choices that are aligned with the Divine.

The 4th Jewel of Awakening is discovered in the depth of your **Heart Chakra.** Your heart can be understood as a Sacred Chalice of Divine Love. As you cultivate the principles of divine consciousness within, such as compassion, love, forgiveness and oneness, your heart opens and receives more and more God Light.

The 5th Jewel of Awakening is the center for Truth and Miracles, related to the **Throat Chakra** and connected to your will power. When your will power is aligned with your higher intention and potential you reach for a higher good in your life, a deeper connection with your sacred source. You take responsibility for your soul's evolution and make choices that support your well-being.

The 6th Jewel of Awakening is Harmony and Clarity, related to the **Third Eye Chakra.** This is the awakening of your inner being, and your ability to perceive truth in connection with Divine Source. The universal principles of truth are activated when this inner Jewel shines. When you are aligned with your path of light, the light of this center becomes a strong guiding force leading you on a path of clear choices, discernment, divine order and beauty.

The 7th Jewel of Awakening is a diamond frequency of Integration and Unity Consciousness, related to the **Crown Chakra.** Through your soul's evolution you come to know that you are truly an expression of Divine Source. The **Crown Chakra** opens to a channel for Divine Guidance and is a bridge between your physical body and your higher self. When this Jewel shines brightly it brings to you the qualities of innocence, purity, sparkling joy and love of life.

In this eternal moment, you are well, free, and in touch with the magic of your being. It is a place of deep peace and joy, and a place that you truly can call home. Deep within each of us is a treasure-chest full of wonder, light, joy, innocence and hope. It is the source of divine power, wisdom, guidance and a deep peace. This place of innocence cannot be touched by negative beliefs or conditioning rooted in fear – for it is the holy center within, protected by the laws of divine love.

Enjoy your Magical Journey!

Wish Fulfilling Tree

A man was sitting under the shade of the Wish Fulfilling Tree. He wished to be a king, and in an instant he became a king. The next moment he wished to have a beautiful damsel with him, and the damsel was instantly by his side. The man then thought within himself, that it is a remote area and is near a forest – what if a tiger came and devoured him. Lo and alas! In an instant he was in the jaws of a tiger!

Similarly, God is like that Wish Fulfilling Tree. Whosoever in God's presence thinks that he is destitute and poor remains as such, but one who thinks and believes that God will fulfill all his desires, receives everything from the Lord. So, from the God, whatever is asked for, God provides to His devotee. God is so kind that He provides everything to His devotee even before asking as God reads the mind of His devotee. If you have firm faith in God and your wish is pure then God shall certainly fulfill your wish.

So, it is very necessary that we have a firm faith in God and we have positive affirmations in our mind. Every thought we have in our mind and every word we say is an affirmation. Let's always have positive thoughts in our mind so that the Wish Fulfilling Tree called God, can fulfill our life with all the positive things. Let's never have negativity in our life or in our thoughts as the same shall then be present in our life. Do not let the tiger of negativity devour you. Let positivity always be on your mind and in your life.

Author Unknown

"*It is* the supreme elixir that overcomes the sovereignty of death.

"*It is* the inexhaustible treasure that eliminates poverty in the world.

"*It is* the supreme medicine that quells the world's disease.

"*It is* the tree that shelters all beings wandering and tired on the path of conditioned existence.

"*It is* the universal bridge that leads to freedom from unhappy states of birth.

"*It is* the dawning moon of the mind that dispels the torment of disturbing conceptions."

– ShantiDeva

Just below the heart chakra is a tiny lotus of 8 petals, the Anandakanda Lotus, within which is the "celestial wishing tree". This magic tree, in front of which is a jeweled altar, is said to hold the deepest wishes of the heart- not what we think we want, but the deeper cries of the soul within. It is believed that when we truly wish upon this tree, and release those wishes, it bestows even more than desired, leading to freedom."

Anodea Judith

The Auras & Energy Fields

*The enlightened give thanks for what most people take for granted.
As you begin to be grateful for what most people take for granted,
that vibration of gratitude makes you more receptive to good in your life.*
– Michael Beckwith

The word "Aura" comes from the Greek word, Avra, meaning breeze. You are a multi-dimensional human being. The spheres of energy surrounding the physical body progressively spiral outward forming our luminous energy fields. Our journey begins in a physical body – the vehicle to fully realize that within us lives a divine and eternal soul. Our inner being uses this vehicle to explore not only what it is to be human, but also what it is to be divine. Our Spirit or Divine nature is simply living life through us, and our work is to allow this miracle to unfold. Our purpose here in this life is to remember who we are in truth. It is the remembering of our true unchanging nature that transcends our temporary life stories.

Your Energy Fields

The Etheric Field is the blueprint of the physical body. It is the first band of energy, a luminous light that surrounds the physical body, protecting and shielding it from outside influences. The Etheric Field is also called the health aura because it emanates strong or weak streams of vital force according to the well-being of the individual. The aura reveals the state of the Etheric field of the individual through its colors and levels of radiance.

The Field of Emotions – The emotional field is the next layer of the aura and it is the source of our feelings and life vitality. When our emotional field is contaminated by negative thinking it is the source of our unhappiness. When our emotional field is nurtured by positive thoughts, intentions and healing affirmations, it reflects our joyous and vibrant well-being.

When we focus our attention on unresolved issues in the past, or we project our thoughts into the future, it results in sadness, depression and anxiety. It is through the divine practice of being in the moment, and keeping our attention on our daily life that we attain a clarity and peace of being.

The three lower chakras hold the keys to our spiritual growth. When we feel fear (Root Chakra) we can transform that energy by affirming trust and gratitude. When we feel unloved or abandonment (Navel Chakra) we can transform that energy into creative physical expression and love of self; reawakening our inner child nature. When we feel disempowered (Solar Plexus Chakra) we can affirm our connection with our source, and surrender to a higher will and life purpose.

Vibrant Well-Being Through Chakra Transformation

The Chakras hold the key to our well-being, opening doorways to our full potential. Each chakra holds the key to our transformation. When they are transcended we are in a steady stream of well-being.

Root Chakra: Fear is transcended through life affirmations of trust, gratitude and intention to serve.

Navel Chakra: Guilt, lack of creative expression and abandonment are transcended to self-acceptance, creativity and love of self.

Solar Plexus: Shame and lack of self-confidence are transcended to self-confidence, surrender and right use of will aligned with source.

Heart Chakra: Sadness and sorrow are transcended to unconditional love of self and others, compassion and joy with the inner work of releasing the past.

Throat Chakra: Suppression of truth and unexpressed potential are transcended to empowerment through truthful speech and ability to listen.

Third Eye Chakra: Unclarity and misunderstandings are transcended to clear seeing, intuition and peaceful understanding.

Crown Chakra: Confusion and lack of direction are transcended to integration, unity and deep guidance from Spirit.

- Divine Consciousness – Crown
- Intuitional Plane – Third Eye
- Buddhic Plane – Throat
- Mental Plane – Heart
- Astral Plane – Solar Plexus
- Etheric Plane – Navel
- Physical Plane – Root

The Mental Field – The Energy of Belief & Source of Higher Wisdom

The mental field exists slightly beyond the emotional body. This is the energy field where our affirmations, intentions, the spoken word, our choices and positive thoughts play an important part in our healing and wellness process. When there are patterns of imbalance in the mental field stemming from negative thinking we are more susceptible to illness. The energy of the mental field is constantly changing, moving rhythmically in response to thought. Remembering how thoughts play an important role in how you are feeling, always choose a better feeling thought!

The Causal Field – The Temple of Our Soul

The causal, celestial or intuitional field – the temple of our true essence – extends beyond the mental field about eighteen inches in an ovoid shape that surrounds the physical field. The energy of this field is radiant and full of color according to our soul's development. The more evolved we become, the more luminous the colors of this energy field. The causal field holds the essence of our higher intuition and is also known as the celestial field because it is composed of the vibrations of our soul's light and wisdom. It is the field that expresses unity and integration with our body and soul.

The Akashic Records

Akasha means "ether" and our souls' records are located in the causal field. These records reveal our journey throughout incarnations and hold the key information regarding our potential, our souls' gifts. We are ever-evolving in love and goodness into higher vibrations of the God Light. As we evolve we hold and stabilize the soul's qualities of unconditional love, joy, harmony and peace.

Crown	Unity
Third Eye	Clarity
Throat	Truth
Heart	Love
Solar Plexus	Empowerment
Navel	Creativity
Root	Trust

"Kundalini Shakti is the coiled energy depicted as a snake moving through the Root Chakra and ending at the Crown Chakra. It is the hidden positive energy of every human being and awakens through your spiritual transformation."

Kundalini - Life Force Energy

Kundalini is the rising or awakening of our life force from its latent state. The root word, Kundal, means to coil, depicting a snake-like energy which lies dormant at the base of the spine in the root chakra. When Kundalini begins to awaken, its purifying fire clears our core light channel or Sushumna Channel. Kundalini is stimulated through all forms of yoga, meditation, energy medicine techniques, the creative arts and nature.

Shiva and Shakti - Unity of Duality

Shakti depicts our creative life force or prana and the ever changing energy of matter. Shiva depicts our unchanging, unlimited, infinite pure consciousness. Shiva and Shakti are ultimately two different sides of the same coin, the all-one divine consciousness. When Kundalini Shakti, the rising creative force, is awakened it begins to travel up the Sushumuna channel, located along the spinal column. It is the desire of Shakti, the energy of Creation, to be reunited with Shiva, the energy of Spirit. This longing becomes the catalyst for the transcendence of the lower chakras. As Shakti travels upward, it disentangles the knots of each chakra which allows them to blossom. When each chakra opens it imparts aspects of our selves that are calling for transformation. A tremendous cosmic unity is experienced when Kundalini Shakti merges with its counter, Shiva. This awakening of true love and wisdom is fully realized in the Crown Chakra and then lays to rest in the temple of the heart. With all chakras open and fully energized the journey is complete and all our experiences are integrated transcending time, space and form.

The Seven Chakras - Your Inner Jewels

The chakras (meaning wheels of light) are whirling centers of vital energy. Each is shaped like a vertical cone. The chakras are seeded in the Sushumna Channel. Chakras function as storage centers – they energize, control and are responsible for proper functioning of our body, mind and emotions. Our life energy flows in an interweaving channel from the Root Chakra up the spine to the Crown Chakra and where it crosses it forms a chakra. These energy centers give the appearance of a brilliant lotus with unfolding petals. When the chakras are blended and integrated they are instruments of divine power and glory. In a state of illumination the chakras are like jewels strung upon the necklace of the Sushumna Channel.

There are seven major chakras – four in the body, and three in the head. There are also many minor chakras throughout the body, as well as the higher spiritual chakras above the head and the mother earth chakra below the feet.

The seven major chakras have a close correspondence to the endocrine glands and are related to the major organs. They play an important part in nourishing and sustaining the nervous system, organs and glands. The chakras also have a direct relationship to our emotions and our belief system, offering us keys to our evolution as spiritual beings. The chakras function as communicators or transmitters of energy from one energy field to another, working in unison to provide the most optimal condition for awakening. The first three chakras – Root, Navel and Solar Plexus – are related to earth, water and fire. The Heart Chakra is related to the element air, the Throat Chakra to light and the Third Eye and Crown Chakras are related to the integration of all elements, making up the spiritual and divine aspect of our being.

Muladhara

Journey Through the Foundation of Our Being

"If you seek the grace of God with your whole heart,
then you may be assured that the grace of God is also seeking you."
– Sri Ramana Maharshi

1st Jewel
Root Chakra
Our Ground of Being

I have stability & abundance in my life

Thhhe first chakra, Muladhara, meaning "SUPPORT AT THE ROOT," is the keeper of our beginnings in this world and the bearer of our foundation. It is located at the base of the spine. This chakra is a whirling vortex of energy flowing into the reproductive organs. It energizes the sexual organs and externalizes as adrenal glands, governing the spine and kidneys. Kundalini, the serpent fire, resides here. The Root Chakra is related to the physical and etheric field subtle bodies, with the element of Earth and the sense of smell.

The Root Chakra provides us with keys to our life purpose. In the Root center we hold the information about our family of origin and ancestral memories. The home of our basic instincts, the Root Chakra drives us to find sexual unity, passion and the fire of life. This fire gives stability, power and the instinct to survive. Our Root deepens our relationship with joy and gratitude for being alive.

In order to maintain balance, the Root Chakra must be in harmony with the Third Eye and Crown Chakras. When we work with the higher centers in our transformation process we create a new sense of grounding. Integration of our lower three chakras with the chakras of our soul, reconnects us with our divine purpose in life. The Crown center brings a security that is everlasting as it connects us with the divine creator of life. The Third Eye center brings our clear vision and connects us with the wisdom to tell the real from the unreal.

Yoga Postures: Bridge Pose, Full Locust, Head to Knee Pose

When this center is balanced, one has developed a deep trust in life. They honor life with gratitude and understand life's changing ebb and flow. Their life energy is intact and they have a reverence for Mother Nature.

Svadhisthana

Journey Through the Sea of Our Emotions

There is nothing you cannot be, or do, or have.
– Abraham Hicks

2nd Jewel
Navel Chakra
Energy & Confidence

I open myself to my fullest potential of my creativity & expression

The second chakra, Svadhistana, meaning "DWELLING IN THE PLACE OF SWEETNESS," is known for where the sea of our emotions reside. It is located at the midpoint of the sacrum. This chakra externalizes as the reproductive glands and governs the reproductive system. The Navel Chakra is related to the etheric field subtle body, and the element of Water with the sense of hearing.

The life force circulates from this chakra with the purpose of nurturing the physical creative force. Energy comes into the field through the spleen and then is distributed to the remaining chakras.

When in balance, the Navel Chakra creates a sense of abundance and appreciation for what life brings. This chakra is considered the seat of Shakti, where our physical, sexual and creative energy is expressed. It is the place of life, conception, change and movement. It can be visualized as a bright sphere of radiant orange light bringing forth creative energies and ideas. This chakra holds the magical wonder of our being and is related to the ages of eight to fourteen, when we most experience life's sweetness and unconditional joy.

The Navel Chakra represents change, duality, movement, flexibility and creative flow. When we energetically tune into this center we can observe that life is best served when we allow ourself to experience it in an unconditional manner.

The energy of the Navel Chakra works closely with the Ajna, or Third Eye Chakra.

Yoga Postures: Leg Lifts, Triangle, Cobra, Spinal Twist

When this chakra is balanced, there are harmonious and connected feelings in one's life. One has healthy sexual feelings, creative expression, and is considerate and friendly with others. One exudes healthiness and vibrancy, has a good self-esteem and positive relationships.

Manipura

Journey Through the Center of Our Power

Transforming yourself is a means of
giving light to the whole world.
– Ramana Maharshi

3rd Jewel
Solar Plexus Chakra
Courage & Strength

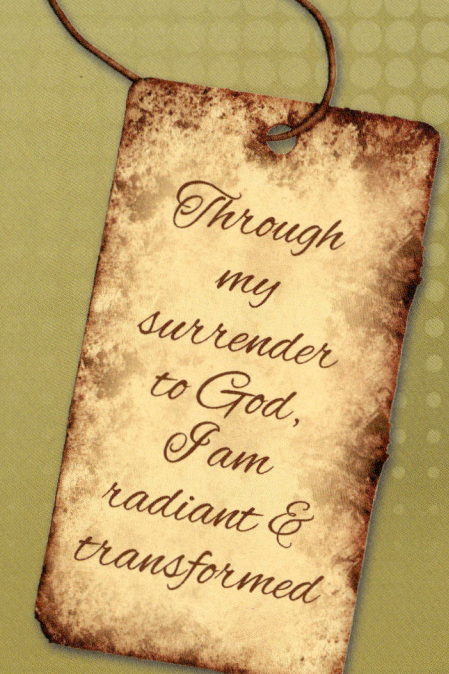

Through my surrender to God, I am radiant & transformed

The third chakra, Manipura, meaning "CITY OF JEWELS," is known for being our power center. It is located between our navel and sternum. The Solar Plexus Chakra receives and distributes energy throughout the physical form. This chakra corresponds to the liver, kidneys and large intestine. The Solar Plexus Chakra is related to the astral and emotional field subtle bodies, with the element of Fire and the sense of sight. Because Manipura is the power center of the physical field, where instincts and survival play an important role, it is easily exhausted. Modern society works through the Solar Plexus Chakra. People are conditioned to fulfill desires, seek personal power and build a false sense of self. The Solar Plexus is our guide to the world around us and provides us with an important protective force until our inner light becomes completely balanced.

The energy of the Solar Plexus Chakra is linked deeply with the heart. The goal of this chakra is to transcend our personal self, and allow ourselves to connect with the inherent unity in life and the true wisdom that comes with this knowing. As we let go of our personal striving, the lotus of the Solar Plexus turns from pointing downward to pointing upward to the heart, forming a bridge of light that assists the lower chakras to unite with the higher.

A journey into our Heart Chakra is an experience of peace and calmness.

Yoga Postures: Bow, The Boat, Sun Salutation

When this center is balanced, there is a feeling of peace and harmony with one's inner self. Actions are performed with a deep reverence for life; light and energy are expressed. Wishes can magically fulfill spontaneously because of the emission of light that the individual gives.

Anahata

Journey Through the Heart of Our Wisdom

Perfect love casts out fear.
– Course in Miracles

4th Jewel
Heart Chakra
Sacred Chalice of Infinite Love

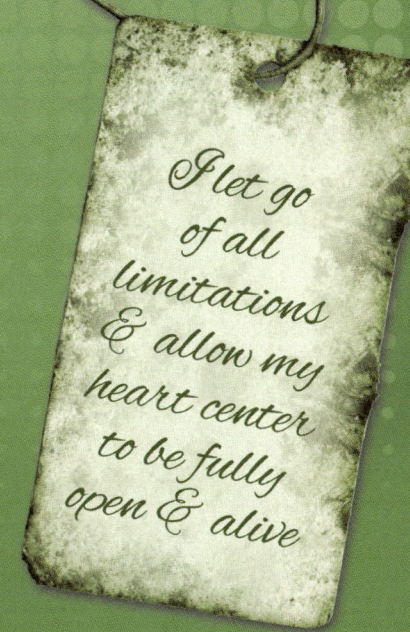

I let go of all limitations & allow my heart center to be fully open & alive

The fourth chakra, Anahara, meaning "UNSTRUCK," is the source of all light and love. It is located in the center of the chest and is where the lower chakras and the higher chakras meet and become integrated, creating oneness of being. The Heart Chakra is related to the mental field subtle body, and the element of Air with the sense of touch. The Heart Chakra is a bridge of light between the lower centers and the higher. All must cross this bridge to move from the limited consciousness of personality to divine consciousness.

The Heart center opening demonstrates the deepest action of love turned inward. The Heart Chakra functions to protect, heal and bring balance to the body, mind and emotions. Because this chakra is closely associated with the thymus gland, which governs the immune system, it is quite vulnerable to our overall level of health. The Heart Chakra awakens us to the qualities of love, forgiveness and compassion helping to release the painful memories of the past. The forgiveness process opens the door to true compassion for our life and our relationships and creates the miracle of understanding. The Heart Chakra opens when the personal will is transformed to divine will and personal power evolves to an empowered heart devoted to peace, giving and receiving love and the practice of discernment. Unconditional love, compassion towards others and ourselves replaces self-centered desire and want. Cherishing our sacred energy, we give from our overflowing heart.

When our heart and spirit are integrated we manifest a life of beauty and joy. Our Heart center is our emotional center where we transform our life through Divine Love. Breathing deeply, allow this Divine Love to open your heart and heal your life!

Yoga Postures: Cobra, Fish, Full Bridge, Camel, Sun Salutation

When this center is balanced, all centers are in harmony. There is a feeling of unconditional love and surrender to a higher will. There is a radiance of love, sincerity, compassion and a deep feeling of wholeness.

Visuddha

Journey Through the Center of Miracles

Let silence speak to you about
the secrets of the universe.
– Rumi

5th Jewel
Throat Chakra
Truth & Miracles

I listen & I am open to life's miracles

The fifth chakra, Visuddha, meaning "PURE PLACE," is the chakra of purification and miracles. It is located at the base of the neck. The Throat Chakra governs the vocal chords, bronchia, lungs and digestive tract and externalizes as the thyroid and parathyroid glands, which metabolize the energy of the system. The Throat Chakra is related to the buddhic subtle body, with the element of Ether and the sense of hearing. It is called the chakra of miracles for its connection with the powers of life and its ability to express clear intentions through the spoken word.

The journey of consciousness takes us through the limitations of the lower chakras into the higher centers of our true self. In the realm of the Throat Chakra, Visuddha, we have the opportunity to express the joy of pure beingness through the voice. The Throat center teaches us to use sound, prayer and affirmations for healing and balancing any discord of our body, mind and emotions. The highest expression of the Throat Chakra is prayer, when one communes with their true self and God. Prayer develops a deep devotion and surrender to the highest will of the divine.

The Throat Chakra is the primary center of healing and transformation of ourselves. When this center is balanced, we express the truth of our authentic self which creates an opening for the grace of healing to take place.

Yoga Postures: Neck Rolls, Fish Pose, Shoulder Stand, The Plough

When this chakra is balanced, an individual expresses thoughts, feelings and emotions without fear. One is honest with themselves and others. Speech is clear, reflecting inner truth. Silence is easily practiced.

Ajna

Journey Through the Center of Clear Perception

The eye with which I see God
is the same eye with which God sees me.
– Meister Eckhart

6th Jewel
Third Eye Chakra
Harmony & Clarity

I am filled with light & trust my intuition

The sixth chakra, Ajna, meaning "COMMAND," is the center of higher intuition. It is located between the eyebrows on the forehead. The Third Eye Chakra is related to the intuitive field subtle body, with the element of Ether and our sixth sense of inner sight.

Our sixth sense, clairvoyance, is developed in the Third Eye Chakra. The related endocrine glands are the pineal and pituitary glands. It governs the eyes, teeth, sinuses, lower brain and the brain stem. When aligned with the soul it brings clear thinking and vision, intuition and truth. When balanced, this center gives the profound ability for one to manifest what they visualize in their life. When one opens this chakra, it merges the dual nature of life so it becomes unified and whole.

This is the master for all the other chakras. The opening of the Ajna is vitally important to achieving full potential in our lifetime. Quieting the mind, deep contemplation and inquiry into the nature of the true self are the paths to accomplishing this opening. This center, when fully awakened, has the power to transform all conditions of our life, which releases karmic patterns from the past and heals the body, mind and emotions. This chakra is awakened through meditation, where we become a vehicle to rest in the light of our pure consciousness.

Yoga Posture: Palming the Eyes, Meditation, Yoga Mudra, Fish

When this chakra is balanced, there is a developed level of perception and one is able to tune in to their inner voice. One is able to attain the gift of visualization and the ability to comprehend life intuitively.

Sahasrara

Journey into Unity Consciousness

To see the world in a grain of sand
and heaven in a wildflower
to hold infinity in the palm of your hand
and eternity in an hour.
– William Blake

7th Jewel
Crown Chakra
Diamond Frequency
Perception & Clarity

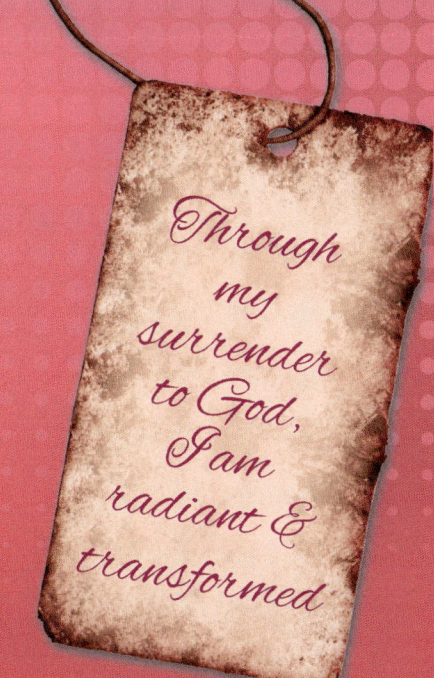

Through my surrender to God, I am radiant & transformed

The seventh chakra, Sahassara, meaning "THOUSAND-PETALED LOTUS," is the chakra of unity. It is located on the crown of the head. It governs the brain and nervous system and externalizes as the pituitary and pineal gland. The Crown Chakra is related to the divine field subtle body, and the element of Cosmic Energy with the sense of thought. Through union and harmony of the Heart and Crown Chakras, love, will, and intelligence are balanced.

This exquisite white thousand-petaled lotus forms a beautiful crown on the head, with the Antahkarana or stem of the flower reaching upward toward the heavens. This stem is the bridge of light between our limited personality and our soul's divine energy. It is the soul's point of entry and exit into this human form and it is also the receiving and distributing station for our life force. The Crown Chakra is activated through our yearning to unite with our inner true nature.

Opening the Crown Chakra allows the divine to clear past impressions and to create an unconditional relationship to life based on the present. Jesus said, "Empty thyself and I shall fill thee," which implies a divine energy entering through the Crown. When we empty ourselves of the scars and conditioning of the past we are born anew into the light.

Yoga Postures: Half-lotus, Headstand, Meditation

When this center is balanced, one has transcended their belief that they are separate from God and has surrendered to the Divine presence within. They are in harmony with life and have acceptance of all that is.

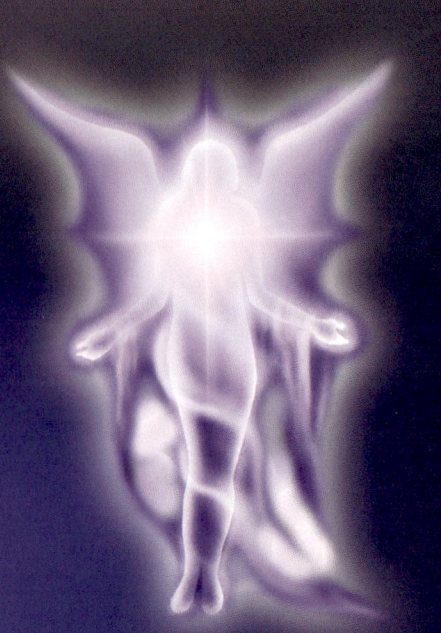

High Self-Meditation

You are a Being of Light!

As a Being of Light, you have a Halo of Divinity that surrounds you with Angelic protection. Within your Halo exists your higher chakras which function as gateways to your Divine Source and portals for Sacred Guidance.

When asking for Guidance you are invited to place your hand on your heart, while focusing your attention on the higher chakras. When your heart and mind are of one-pointed intention, you are on the path of reaching your highest potential.

Begin by taking slow, deep breaths. Breathing out, release unwanted stresses and worries. Breathing in, you will feel an expanded sense of self and well-being.

Now focus your attention above your head and visualize a tube of light connected from Spirit to your Crown Chakra. This tube of light is the channel which divine energies pour through and impress upon you the whispers of angelic guidance. A deep peace will come over you as you ask for guidance, letting go of any resistance and see your life unfolding for the highest good.

Always end your connection with Spirit with deep gratitude; knowing, feeling, believing and manifesting your request from the Universe.

Your Sacred Energy

Your Sacred Energy comes from the Source that animates every living thing. All of creation is made up of this mysterious energy vibrating at different frequencies. All of life is connected through the web of Creation, blessed by the Divine Plan to evolve in Love and Consciousness.

We begin to understand that everything is energy and that we are deeply interconnected and guided to not only take care of our physical bodies but to pay attention to our thoughts and feelings as well. We also realize that our connection to the universal Spirit or God Light is the source of our joy. We are evolving to greater and greater capacity to receive and express the Spiritual Light and Love of the Creator.

The Heart Initiation

When the heart initiation takes place we enter into our Buddhic light, the vehicle of our soul. The principles of higher consciousness are now the foundation for our being, as our personal will is now surrendered to the will of God. Through this initiation, Kundalini energy is unleashed to move freely from its resting place at the base of the spine upward to the Sahasrara chakra at the crown of the head. This movement of our life force is the marriage of matter and spirit. The Shakti force at the base of the spine meets the Shiva force at the crown center flowing together into the heart center. Through this union we become soul-infused beings, creating a deep sense of wholeness.

Through the heart initiation, we attain the essence of balance and equanimity within, and are no longer affected by the duality of life. The great downpour of sacred energy occurs from the upper chakras, flooding the lower chakras with divine energy. The heart initiate is tested in every degree to free the heart from past inclinations toward lust, hate, greed, pride and envy, so that there may be freedom from selfishness. Through the opening up of the heart center we become spiritual warriors, protecting our sacred energy from the pitfalls of illusion. Harmlessness is cultivated. The symbol for the heart chakra is the deer, achieving ahimsa, the path of peace in daily life. As does this gentle deer, the aspirant places his complete trust in God.

The heart center opening can be painful. It is the cross that we must bear when leaving our identification with the temporary nature of life. Through the cleansing of our emotional, and the release of the past, the heart center opens. The luminous gateway of our heart center leads to the antahkarana or bridge of light, which makes the ascension back to our true home possible. This sacred bridge is energetically constructed through a complete letting go of spiritual ignorance and identification with a separate sense of self. The heart chakra center is the master station for the polarities of the emotional, mental and etheric bodies. The lower impulses of the chakras of the personality are mastered and transformed to reflect our true essence of divinity. Through initiation into the heart chakra, qualities like reverence, service, compassion and selfless love are developed.

In the centre of the castle of Brahman, our own body, there is a small shrine in the form of a lotus-flower, and within can be found a small space. We should find who dwells there, and we should want to know him.

And if anyone asks, "Who is he who dwells in a small shrine in the form of a lotus-flower in the centre of the castle of Brahman? Whom should we want to find and to know?" we can answer~ "The little space within the heart is as great as this vast universe. The heavens and the earth are there, and the sun, and the moon, and the stars, fire and lightning and winds are there, and all that now is and all that is not...for the whole universe is in Him and He who dwells within our heart."

Chandogya Upanishad

The Lotus of the Heart *Om Mane Padme Hum*

The lotus of the heart unfolds deeply as we turn our attention inward, realizing our true nature is pure witness consciousness. Our true nature is always present watching, observing and waiting silently in the seat of our heart. Through the process of letting go of the false self, held in separation and personal power, our heart opens to its natural flowering. Each of the twelve petals of consciousness unfolds as we become aligned with our soul.

1st petal unfolds when we meet our innermost self within the sanctuary of our heart, and awareness turns from identification with the body to knowing our true self.

2nd petal unfolds through realization that we are not our emotions nor our mind. Our true nature is an expression of divinity, found in the heart of goodness, in alignment with inner truth.

3rd petal unfolds in the lotus of the heart, when our thinking is used for higher aspiration, and the mind becomes silent. The mind, having dissolved into the sacred heart, becomes a silent observer and our thoughts transform to intuition, perception and discernment.

4th petal unfolds when we release attachment to the things of this world. The knowledge obtained within our heart's unfolding lotus deepens our understanding of pure consciousness.

5th petal unfolds when we are firmly embedded into our true nature, demonstrating steadfastness, vigilance and uncompromising clarity.

6th petal unfolds when all that is not of our pure consciousness is burned in the sacred fire of our inner light.

7th petal unfolds when our inner being is adorned with all inclusive love, harmlessness and devotion to the ever-present sacred self that resides in the spiritual heart.

8th petal unfolds when there is a direct perception of our true reality. All doubt is removed from seeing the light of consciousness.

9th petal unfolds when there is deep and profound peace; the past is dissolved completely and our true freedom has been realized.

10th petal unfolds when we live fully in each sacred moment, awaiting life's calling to service.

11th petal unfolds when we experience the joy of our being and share it with others.

12th petal unfolds when we walk the path of compassion.

Soul Star

Soul Star Chakra - Transpersonal Center
Portal for Ascension also known as the Stellar Gateway.
Through this gateway, Divine light energy flows through the
Crown Chakra and then is distributed through the body.

8th Jewel
Soul Star

White – Divine Guidance

Color White for Soul Star • Silver for Earth Star
Gemstone- Stone White Selenite, Clear Quartz
Earth Star Grounding Stones -Smokey Quartz

I awaken my light body with wisdom, love & truth

The Soul Star Chakra is located about 4 to 5 inches above the head. This chakra is the center in which you receive universal inspiration and divine guidance. The Soul Star when harmonized expresses divine love, will and wisdom. This spiritual center holds infinite potential for enlightenment and transcendence. It is through deep surrender and letting go that we connect with our higher self and open this channel to receive divine guidance.

The Soul Star Chakra has its exact duplicate below the feet, known as the Earth Star Chakra – silver in color, and is known as the Terra Chakra. It provides the energy of deep grounding and connection to earth and it is a receptive energy, containing all the elements of earth, wind, fire and water.

Understanding our connection with our divine purpose in physical form and our spiritual awakening is an art that can be mastered through balancing and alignment of our entire chakra system. The Terra Chakra assists us in understanding our sacred earth contract and our unique life purpose while our Soul Star Chakra holds our potential as spiritual beings on a path of evolution.

Soul Star & Earth Star Meditation

Imagine yourself in a bubble of light that is surrounding you from the top of your head (your Soul Star) to below your feet (your Earth Star). Breathing deeply, visualize the light from the Soul Star traveling down through your head, through your body and deeply connecting with your Earth Star. As it travels, pay attention to any areas of your energy fields that could use support. Allow the light from your Soul Star to focus its healing energy where you may need attention. The light will do the work. Breathing out, let go of any constriction, pain or other resistance. Breathing in, allow the light to balance, harmonize, heal and bring peace to your life. Now focus your attention on the Earth Star Chakra, below your feet. Take a moment in deep prayer and send an affirmation of gratitude and affirm your life purpose as a being of light ready to offer service where needed.

Soul Purpose

Soul Purpose Chakra - The God Portal

The Divine Template of your Soul's Journey
and where we receive angelic guidance.

9th Jewel
Soul Purpose

Violet ~ Angelic Guidance

I welcome my soul's purpose as a being of love, light & beauty

The ninth Chakra, or *God Portal Chakra,* is located about 12 inches above the head and is blue and violet - ultra violet in color. This chakra is known to hold the Divine Template of your Soul's Journey which is in essence the keeper of your Spiritual Gifts. The Soul Purpose Chakra holds the information about your Akashic Records and it is also the chakra where we receive angelic guidance. When this center has awakened, you become a truly multi-dimensional being and your work will be to assist others in their awakening.

The function of this chakra is the access of information about Karma, lessons, our learning abilities, doorways to other dimensions and times, as well as the Akashic records. It is through this chakra that we view past life information. Occasionally we can obtain this information in the dream state, when there is important information to communicate to us. Often spirit/angels will use our dreams to get our attention. The dream state many times expresses ideas in symbols and it is our job to interpret the symbols presented. We can, of course, gain confirmation of our interpretation through meditation.

Soul Purpose Meditation

Turning within, take a moment to breathe and listen to the whispers of your angelic guidance. Ask your angelic guidance a question about your life path, one that is important to you. Being very quiet, listen and wait for sensations in your body, especially your Solar Plexus center. The answer to your questions will often appear as sensations of deep peace, joy, excitement and vision that supports your life path. This is the way the angels communicate.

When this chakra is balanced there is a feeling of ease and grace. You feel like you have a angelic companion in life, guiding you through feelings of joy, peace and love throughout your day.

10ᵗʰ Jewel

Destiny Chakra

Gold – Divine Service

I am a timeless being of ever-evolving love

The Destiny Chakra, or *Grand Portal Chakra*, is located about 18 inches above the head and is gold in color. This is the chakra believed to be the pathway for soul travel into other parts of the universe including higher dimensions.

This is the chakra where true integration of polarities have occurred and you are now in complete equilibrium. When this chakra is completely open you are in a perpetual state of receiving high universal energy and have become a master whose life is dedicated to Divine service.

The Angelic Chakra contains the programming of the soul for this lifetime and the history of the soul. It is through our connection and understanding of this chakra that we gain (or affect) our own healings and insights. We also learn our lessons, understand the soul contracts and begin to understand our life purpose.

Destiny Meditation

I am open to the universe's teaching. I simply ask "What am I to do" and "I allow life to bring me experiences and doorways to take me to my full potential. I affirm that my life is about Divine service and ask that all my actions be devoted to this purpose."

When this chakra is balanced there is a deep feeling of oneness with all of life. You walk the middle road, between the experiences of good and bad, pleasure and pain and you hold a deep peace within your heart that is not affected by outer circumstances.

The Art of Meditation

Meditation is a state of communion with the divine – the pure essence of God within our heart. When the mind dissolves into the heart of stillness, it is possible to see the divine in all of creation. This gives space for the mind to be born anew and be purified from the past, leading ultimately to peace and freedom of being. Our true nature lives in each moment, is reborn in the next moment, and is constantly dying to the old. This renewal process of each moment requires us to practice letting go through our breath. With each inhale, we allow ourselves to become immersed in *What Is*- the true vastness of being. With each exhale, we surrender our sense of separation. Through deep inner silence, we experience a unity in life, where all is laid to rest in the peace of the sacred force that is always present.

Five Steps to Meditating with Ease

1. Create a Sacred Space
Your meditating space should be free of clutter, electronics or distracting stimulus. You may want to bring a candle, crystals or other sacred objects to the space. Bring pillows and blankets so you can sit in comfort. Quiet spots in nature are also very conducive to meditation.

2. Find a Comfortable Seat
You can sit cross-legged in easy pose, lotus or hero's pose. You may want to sit on a pillow; this will assist in allowing your hip flexors to relax. Sit with a long spine and lower your shoulders away from your ears. You may want to sit against a wall to help your spine stay erect. Doing some light stretches prior to your meditation practice can help you sit with more comfort. See page,49 Daily Chakra Exercises, for some suggestions on exercises.

3. Set a Regular Time
Try to set a consistent time everyday for your meditation practice. The best times to meditate are at dawn or dusk, but it is more important that you set a time that works with your schedule. The more regular you can become with your practice, the easier meditation will come and the deeper you will go into silence. You will feel tremendous benefit in your body and mind from practicing meditation for just 10 minutes a day.

Come without memory or premonition.
Come blindly into it.
Sit without resistance.
Let your rampant vibrancy exchange with the abstract and incomprehensible.
Feel the sweet death of being out of control.
There is no ending point.
Your surrender is the infinite language.
You are the co-creator of this uncommon existence.
Dance within the rolling waves.
Fill the sky with your magenta dreams.
Put the world to bed under the crystal night heaven.
The Fairy Tale is yours.

By Arya

Hero's Pose

4. Begin with Breath

Practice full yogic breathing in the beginning of your meditation practice. Inhale deeply for 3 seconds, allowing your belly to expand fully, and exhale for 3 seconds. With each exhale, visualize tension leaving your body and mind. Dedicate the first few minutes of your practice to intentional yogic breathing and then return to your natural state of breathing.

5. Become a Witness

Close your eyes and retreat inward. Allow yourself to detach from your thoughts and impulses. Begin to observe the ebb and flow of your mind. Feel the fullness of your presence by just *Being*. Release anything that pulls you to move out of the stillness and spaciousness of the present moment. Your mind will still do as it always does, but as you retreat into the silence and fullness of your heart, you will find it easier to disengage from your thoughts and rediscover your own Sacred Presence.

*Empty yourself
of everything.
Let the mind become still.
The ten thousand
things rise and fall
while the self
watches their return.
The returning to the
source is stillness,
which is the way
of nature.*

Lao Tsu, Tao Te Ching

The Miracle Prayer

*I open my heart wide to receive the love of God.
As I receive God's love as universal supply,
all my affairs are healed.
I realize and accept the healing power of the
Universe as love, and I allow the healing power
that is love to penetrate my life.
I readily accept the healing power of love
in my life and I know that as love,
God is my limitless and
abundant supply made manifest.
I feel the outpouring of God's love
in my body and mind.
I feel God's love in my affairs,
and I know all is well.*

Journey Through the Chakra's Color Meditation

Begin at the Root Chakra

- Feel the vital energy of the earth as it enters the **Root Chakra,** intensely connecting you with the earth...

- Relax and allow your breath to assist in releasing tensions, worries and anxieties...

- Feel yourself letting go into a deeper and deeper state of peace...

- Breathe gently from your lower abdomen...

- Slowly, deeply, your breath moves throughout your being assisting you in relaxation...

- Let your awareness move to your lower abdomen, the base of the spine where the seat of the **Root Chakra** and the Kundalini reside. This is your grounding center, the foundation of your being...

- Feel a sense of belonging, inner security and trust, knowing that you are on a grand journey of life to the kingdom of your own divinity...

- Your purpose here is to trust, accept and learn the art of being. You have inner security and gratitude for the opportunity this birth brings...

- Visualize a glowing red sun here, nurturing and awakening your vital force within...

- Feel grounded and centered, let go of any insecurity within the sacred life force.

Move up to the Navel

- As your breathing comes into rhythm with the vital energy running up your spine, feel your awareness move to the sacral center, the center of cleansing water that circulates around your abdominal area, cleansing, refreshing and purifying physical and emotional toxins.

- Bring a golden-orange ray of vital energy here, allow your physical creative force to surface, embrace your passion for life and feel the miracle of the vital force within you.

Move up to the Solar Plexus

- As you move from the watery, creative substance of the second chakra into the fiery nature of the **Solar Plexus Chakra,** you feel alive with the flowing, vital current of your being. Embrace your sense of self and feel secure in life's process. Now allow your awareness to enter the fiery solar plexus region, the physical sun of your universe. This is the source of personal power, the chakra of transformation.

- As you move your awareness from personal identification to your true nature of the impersonal self, feel the glowing energy here. The golden color of the Solar Plexus center warms your entire being.

- Your breath takes you into deeper relaxation and ease as you allow any worries or concerns to be dissolved by the fire of the Solar Plexus, bringing a deep sense of peace and abundance.

Know that through the breath you can relax and bring calmness and healing light to all thoughts and emotions.
You are in the center of your radiance.
Allow the personal self to transcend its own sense
of power to the power of divine will.
This requires a surrender of identification held in separation.
Know that you are one unified whole in union
with the divine nature of your being.

Move up to the Heart

- Move from the flaming sea of the Solar Plexus to the gentle harmlessness of the **Heart center,** sensing your integration with light. There is a beautiful color of rose pink here representing unconditional love and a hue of green representing the healing light of the soul.

- You feel the love and compassion deep within your heart.

Move up to the Throat

- Bring this awareness of your true nature as you enter the **Throat Chakra.** The miracle of this center is knowing and expressing your truth so that all things beautiful and true in your life are manifested.

- Feel a light blue radiance here, as you open to the unlimited expansion of perception and divine creativity.

- Allow yourself to discern the truth, express the truth and listen within to the infinite space and unbounded consciousness of your divine essence.

Move up to the Third Eye

- The radiance of this center opens you to deeper levels of truth and you move into the **Third Eye - Ajna** center, the eye of wisdom and stillness, where you access unlimited perception and understanding of life.

- This wisdom center, bathed in indigo light, takes you to the infinite creation.

- You feel receptive and at peace with all of life as you penetrate the stillness of empty space.

- Thoughts dissipate in this stillness as you connect with the sacred force.

Move up to the Crown
- The journey has taken you into the realm of cosmic knowledge, beyond all concepts and thoughts.
- This silence carries you to the home of your true self; you now go into the integration force of the Crown Chakra.
- A brilliant purple light floods down through all your chakras, integrating and bringing their energies into balance.
- You feel unleashed from all the chains of temporary manifestation; you have moved into the eternal, free-flowing energy of the unbounded consciousness of the Crown Chakra.

You have now merged all sense of separation into the omnipresent and radiant light of God.

Color Healing, The Aura and Chakras
The aura and chakra energies work together to create and maintain life.
There are seven colors that correspond to the seven chakras.

Root Chakra
Red: Base chakra, relates to passion, life energy, sexuality and creativity. Stimulated with Green, Indigo and Violet. Soothed by Red, Orange, Yellow and Blue. Red – Life, physical self, physical plane. Energizes vitality, creativity, power and courage. Stimulates nerves.

Navel Chakra
Orange: Sacral (adrenals), relates to physical movement, etheric health, well-being and joy. Stimulated by Red. Calmed by Blue, Yellow. Orange – Health, vital self, physical plane. Healing, wisdom, circulates prana, strengthens etheric.

Solar Plexus Chakra
Yellow: Solar Plexus (nervous system), center of recognition and self-worth. Stimulated by Red, Orange, Yellow, Violet. Calmed by Blue and Indigo. Yellow – Wisdom, emotional plane, power self, self-awakening, inspiring, stimulating, wisdom, digestive process, increases intellect and power of reason.

Heart Chakra
Green: Heart, relates to love, harmony and balance. Stimulated by Red, Orange, Indigo and Violet. Soothed by Yellow, Green and Blue. Green – Energy, healing self, mental plane, whole self, harmony, balance, stimulates heart, releases tension, and negative energies.

Throat Chakra
Blue: Throat, thyroid, relates to creative expression through sound, communication and truth. Stimulated by Red. Calmed by Blue, Indigo, Green and Yellow. Blue – Inspiration, peaceful self, mental plane, healing self. Truth, perfection, devotion, creativity, peace, calming, intuition, connects us with higher mental body.

Third Eye Chakra
Violet: Third Eye (pituitary gland), relates to creative visualization. Gathers instruction from higher self. Indigo – Intuition, inspired self, buddhic plane. Devotion, clarity, expansion of consciousness, cools, strengthens thyroid and parathyroid. Purifies blood stream, heals emotional plane.

Crown Chakra
Magenta: Crown (pineal gland), relates to the eternal, spiritual self, connects us to cosmic consciousness. Violet – Spiritual power, spiritual self, logic plane. Meditation, inspiration. Purifies blood, stops the growth of tumors.

Hand chakras are the centers of awareness of the hands. They are located in the middle of the palms.

Clearing the Chakras Through Your Healing Hands

For clearing the chakras, place your palm chakras above each chakra and move it in counterclockwise motion. This will remove static energy and clear negative build-up. Flick your hands after the motion to remove the energy. After you clear a chakra, move your hand clockwise on the chakra at least one time more than the counter-clockwise movements. The number of these movements depend on how the chakras feel; listen to your intuition.

Note: The chakras are tools for transformation. We balance them through a simple clearing motion (as above), use them to gain understanding of our issues and map our healing course.

Daily Chakra Clearing Meditation

Place your hand, palm turned toward the body, at a distance that feels comfortable to you. Start at just a few inches above the body and then move your hand as far away as you can and still feel sensation/energy from the chakra. Hover over each chakra as you speak or think the following affirmations. You can visualize the color of each chakra as you repeat the affirmation.

Affirmations

1st Root (red) *I am eternally secure. My soul exists through all time.*

2nd Navel (orange) *I love unconditionally. I am one with the divine mother.*

3rd Solar Plexus (yellow) *Power in the center is the core Divine power. I am one with that power and it runs throughout all of my being.*

4th Heart (green) *The river of love flows through my heart and then through my whole body. I am a child of love, present, connected and surrendered to the flow.*

5th Throat (light blue) *My voice is clear and true.*

6th Third Eye (indigo blue) *I see through the illusions to truth.*

7th Crown (pink or violet) *I bring all my learning, gifts and tools from all lifetimes as medicine for the greater good.*

Meditation & Gemstones

Chakra gemstones are fascinating. A lot of people wear them as jewelry, rings and pendants just to help keep the body in balance. But the biggest key to Gemstone healing is of course **meditation**. Most people meditate with their gems in a peaceful quiet spot. They hold the gems gently in their hands and slowly inhale and exhale. Having quiet time and personal space for yourself can help you concentrate deeper and channel your inner chakras better. Some people lay down and place the chakra gemstones and crystals over their body parts so they can transmit their energy forces and vibrations in and out of their bodies like breath.

You can place the gemstones in these areas:

1st Root Chakra - **Place between your Knees**

2nd Navel Chakra - **Place below your Navel**

3rd Solar Plexus Chakra - **Place between your Navel & Rib Cage**

4th Heart Chakra - **Place in the middle of your Chest**

5th Throat Chakra - **Place on your Throat**

6th Third Eye Chakra - **Place on your Forehead**

7th Crown Chakra - **Place on the floor above your Head**

Placing ALL the chakras across your body at the same time will intensify the force and energy you feel. This is a very powerful way of receiving thoughts, feelings and sensations.

Chakra Kinesiology Test

Please review the Kinesiology testing guidelines before performing this chakra test. When you feel confident in your testing skills you can use Kinesiology to determine which chakra is in need of balancing. Remember to always ask your client or friend for permission to test. To begin, place your hand over or above the chakra being tested. It is not necessary to touch the body. For kinesiology guidelines, downloads, and training information see www.jewelsoflight.com for more information.

Begin with one hand over the chakra while the other hand is used to perform the Kinesiology test. First, test the Crown Chakra while asking the question *"Is the Crown Chakra balanced?"* If the answer is Yes – meaning balanced, the arm will stay strong. If the answer is No – meaning unbalanced, the arm will go weak. Do this procedure for each of the chakras.

- **Crown:** At the baby's soft spot. Integration, openness, connection.
- **Third Eye:** Between eyebrows. Perception, right understanding.
- **Throat:** At the throat area. Expression of truth, responsibility.
- **Heart:** Between breastbones. Self-love, integration of mind and emotions.
- **Solar Plexus:** Just below rib cage in the abdomen area above the navel. Emotional nature, integration of power.
- **Navel:** Below belly button. Relationships and self-expression in the world.
- **Root:** At the area of the pubic bone, hold hand above pubic area. Security, groundedness, and trusting in life's process.

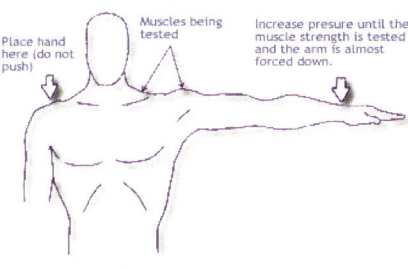

Basics of muscle testing

Energy Evaluation Using the Pendulum

You may find that you prefer to use a pendulum for energy testing instead of muscle testing. One advantage of this method is that you can perform it without the use of your client's arm.

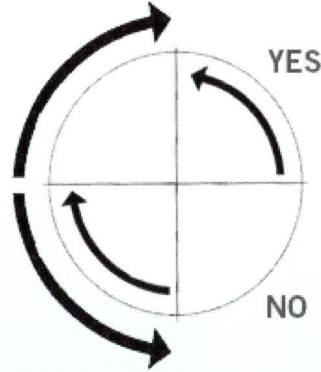

Pendulum use for chakra evaluation

1. When working with the chakras and a pendulum, place the pendulum over or in front of the chakra and observe the way it spins.

2. If pendulum doesn't spin, then the chakra could be inactive or under-energized. It may also spin in a counter-clockwise manner, which indicates that the energy is unbalanced. A clockwise manner should indicate the chakra is fully functioning. You can determine the differences between chakras and notice some are spinning more rapidly than others. These may require some balancing. Through breathing and affirmations you can often bring a particular chakra back into balance.

3. You can also use the pendulum to discover the condition of a chakra by holding it over your palm chakra and asking about each of your chakras in turn.

Breathing Deeply & Chakra Sounds

The chakras are located along the Sushumna channel and are energized by Prana, the Life Force. Our breath greatly affects the functioning of our chakras. The lower back, lower abdomen and pelvic areas carry information about our roots, our family, our origin, our survival needs and our sense of grounding.

Breathing deeply into the Root Chakra helps to keep us feeling grounded and balanced.

The **Navel Chakra** holds information about our sense of self, our relationships, physical energy and creativity.

Breathing deeply, along with deep exhalations, assists our second chakra to stay balanced as well as opens us to our vital force energy.

Our **Solar Plexus Chakra** holds information about how we use our sense of power and helps us unite our mind with our heart.

Breathing deeply relaxes our struggle for personal power.

Our **Heart Center** is our emotional center where we transform our life through Divine Love.

Breathing deeply, allow this Divine Love to open your heart and heal your life!

Our **Throat Chakra** opens as we breathe in and exhale; we feel the current of energy from the lower chakras and direct this energy upward and out the crown center. When this current is flowing freely we can feel confident to speak and walk our truth.

Breathing deeply and exhaling fully allows our full energy to circulate up the chakras and through the crown. Then we feel we are in a circle of vibrant light.

The **Third Eye Chakra** softens and opens as the pranic energy moves up and bathes the inner eye in the warm wind of our breath. The Third Eye Chakra tells the story of who we are and where we came from to help us meet our celestial nature.

The **Crown Chakra** holds the stories of all our births, creates a crown of glory as it opens and connects with the divine source when we breathe deep and exhale through the crown center.

Positive emotions and thoughts such as joy, peace, and contentment sustain our health and well-being. Negative emotions and thoughts create disturbances that affect our energy field eventually leading to disease. We can learn to exhale what is no longer serving us and inhale the qualities and principles of life we need. Breathing deeply creates strength in our energy field and shields us from negative thinking. Breathing with the energy of expanding opens us to our intuitive field and allows us to meet our true nature. The art of breathing holds the key to all processes in healing the body, mind and spirit. Breathing assists us in remaining centered and calm. Through the quiet mind we can choose peace rather than problems or conflict and release personal holdings. Our deep exhalation process provides the tools necessary to surrender the most difficult and challenging experiences.

Remaining conscious of our true nature, remembering who we are, is essential in working with the energy fields. We then can use all of life's experience as a gift to remain in peace and harmony, our intention to live free from personal suffering.

Practice toning daily for optimal well being.

The vibrations of vowel sounds can activate the chakras.

Chakra Healing Sounds:

Root Chakra .... LAM
Navel Chakra ... VAM
Solar Plexus Chakra ... RAM
Heart Chakra ... YAM
Throat Chakra ... HAM
Third Eye Chakra ... KSHAM
Crown Chakra ... OM

- Close your eyes, breathe in through the nose, then out through mouth, allowing the vowel you have chosen to sound.

- Don't intone the vowel loudly. Use a low voice and let it vibrate for as long as you can while remaining relaxed.

- If you intone a vowel for a minute or two and concentrate on the chakra that you want to affect, you will be able to feel how it is animated and activated.

- Repeat for a few minutes to feel the full effect on your body and mind.

Angelic Chakra Meditation

Take a moment to relax, breath and put your worries, concerns and stresses aside. We are now going to invoke the Angels, requesting them to bring healing, balancing and vitality to our chakras.

Begin, by visualizing an angelic white light. Allow this sparkly light to enter the top of your head, through the **Crown Chakra** (baby's soft spot). This chakra is your center for Divine connection and it is always receiving Spiritual wisdom to guide you on your path. Ask the angels to keep this center free from confusion so you have a clear channel to your Divine guidance.

Your Spiritual Light travels down your face with a soothing, healing energy. Feel this energy move down the face through the **Third Eye** (the point between the eyebrows) and allow this frequency to assist you to see your life with a spiritual perspective. This chakra will bring you inner vision, the ability to see clearly and know the truth.

The light continues to travel down to your **Throat Chakra** where you are able to see and speak your truth. This is the *Chakra of Miracles*; the center where your spoken word is very powerful. Ask for guidance to assist you to speak that which is true for you and that which you request from the universe. Feel what you have requested with a deep heart of gratitude. Then, watch your life unfold!

The white light of the angelic realm now travels gently to the **Heart Chakra**, the home of unconditional love and the way of the Christ. Ask for guidance from the angelic realm to assist you in healing any unresolved issues or misunderstandings about love. Know that the love of divine is unconditional love and forgiveness of self. The **Heart Chakra** is your home base, a sacred temple within where you can rest, be attuned to Spirit and reborn into your true nature.

Now, allow this angelic white light to travel down to the **Solar Plexus Chakra,** a place of great energy where your earthly experiences are most felt. Ask your angelic guides to assist you with the deep surrender required from the **Solar Plexus**. As you relax this center you feel an increased sense of peace and well-being.

Next, allow the white angelic light to move into the **Navel Chakra**, the center of life, creation, desire, and passions. Ask your angelic guides to heal and balance your desires and sexual energy to be aligned with your highest good. Affirm a deep acceptance of yourself, releasing all shame and sense of abandonment from this center.

The angelic white light now flows deep into the **Root Chakra**, the foundation of your being. Remember you have a life purpose and you are safe and secure. Ask your divine guidance to reveal to you your unique life purpose and remember your security is found in trusting in Spirit, releasing fear and knowing deeply you have been instilled with the gifts of divine creation.

Chakras in Relationship to Your Health

1. **The Root Chakra** *reflects the conditions of the lower back, spine, kidneys, adrenals, reproductive organs, small intestine, bladder, sciatica, and legs.*

   - Low back pain
   - Sciatica
   - Osteoporosis
   - Varicose veins
   - Constipation
   - Pain in legs and feet
   - Hemorrhoids
   - Anemia/blood disorders
   - Stress induced ailments
   - Digestive disorders
   - Allergic reactions

2. **The Navel Chakra** *reflects your source of energy. Look for signs of distress in the kidneys, adrenals, sexuality and sense of self.*

   - Ulcers/stomach pain
   - Heartburn
   - Jaundice
   - Anorexia
   - Backache
   - Obesity
   - Digestive track disorders
   - Nervous disorders
   - Liver, spleen, gallbladder problems

3. **The Solar Plexus** *shows signs of stress in the digestive process and assimilation of food as well as emotions. The Solar Plexus will reflect tightness due to power issues and sensing the world through feelings.*

   - Menstrual pains
   - Cysts
   - Impotence
   - Kidney stones
   - Prostate problems
   - Hip joint pain
   - Urinary infections
   - Lower back pain
   - Weak bladder
   - Kidney problems
   - Testicular ailments
   - Inflamed ovaries

4. **The Heart Chakra** *imbalances will show as heart weakness, life force blocks, circulation problems, general immune system problems as well as the emotional inability to love oneself, or give or receive love.*

   - Coronary illness
   - Angina
   - Colds/lung infections
   - Asthma
   - Allergies
   - High cholesterol
   - Backache
   - Shoulder pain
   - High/low blood pressure
   - Rheumatism arms/hands
   - Skin problems

5. **The Throat Chakra** *will reflect the metabolic system as well as neck, thyroid, parathyroid, breathing and emotional issues of communication, ability to listen and hear.*

   - Throat pain
   - Tonsillitis
   - Speech defects
   - Dental problems
   - Shoulder/neck pain
   - Thyroid problems
   - Vertebrae pain
   - Stuttering

6. **The Third Eye Chakra** *will reflect imbalances having to do with sight, nervous system and emotional issues of perception and understanding.*

   - Migraine/headaches
   - Neurological disorders
   - Conjunctivitis
   - Schizophrenia
   - Sinus problems
   - Middle ear problems
   - Brain disorders
   - Learning disabilities

7. **The Crown Chakra** *will affect the entire body and show signs of imbalance during any serious disease. Emotionally the crown is related to the integration of life experiences on all levels.*

   - Headaches
   - Immune weakness
   - Paralysis
   - Depression
   - Cancer
   - Sleep disorders
   - Mental confusion
   - Multiple Sclerosis

Aromatherapy Through Chakra Fragrances

Aromatherapy is a gentle healing technique that harmonizes the senses and helps dissolve blockages in the chakras.

Root	*Cloves, Cedar, Jasmine, Rose, Patchouli, Myrrh, Musk*
Navel	*Ylang Ylang, Sandalwood, Jasmine, Rose*
Solar Plexus	*Peppermint, Lemon, Rosemary, Carnation, Lavender, Cinnamon, Marigold, Chamomile, Thyme, Juniper, Vertiver*
Heart	*Attar of Roses, Bergamot, Clary Sage, Geranium, Melissa*
Throat	*Sage, Eucalyptus, Frankincense, Lavender, Sandalwood, Chamomile*
Third Eye	*Rosemary, Juniper*
Crown	*Sandalwood, Jasmine, Rose, Lavender, Frankincense*

Use the earth's energies to balance the chakras or simple visualizations that use nature.

Root Center:
Lotus position sitting on earth. Any connection with the earth will balance the root as well as assist you in grounding your energies.

Navel Center:
Ocean, waterfalls, streams, lakes, ponds and all watery aspects of nature.

Solar Plexus Center:
Sun, fire, desert, heat, all warming aspects of nature.

Heart Center:
Connect with all green aspects of nature.

Throat Center:
Healing through connection with all blue aspects of nature, such as water, skies, etc.

Third Eye Center:
Healing through stargazing and night skies.

Crown Center:
Healing through climbing to high places, mountains.

Balancing the Chakras Through Nature

White Light Energy Protection, Clearing & Grounding

Whenever you feel energetically out of balance, drained, disturbed, negative or depressed, you might consider energy clearing to clear, balance and renew your energy.

Here are some tips to create a strong energy field.

- **Use the light** to create a force field of protection around your body.
- **Create a shield** of white light from your inner energy field, filtering all thought, feelings and emotions that are not of the highest good.
- **Visualize a force field** of white light surrounding and protecting your body. For protection, imagine a mirror around the body. This mirror reflects on the outside pushing away anything from us as if it is reflecting back to the source.
- **Using white candles** and incense, create a sacred space for your daily energy practice, take time to meditate, breathe and align your energy with your source.
- **To ground and center your energy**, imagine a silver cord through your spine, connecting you deep with mother earth.

To clear the aura, imagine you are under a beautiful blue waterfall. Allow the water to flow through your Crown Chakra, through your inner energy field and off your feet, clearing all unwanted accumulated energy.

Applications

- The best way to use oils is to put a few drops in an aroma lamp.
- You can also use essential oils in a bath or foot bath and in combination with chakra-massage techniques.
- Palm Chakras: Put in center of palms of hands.
- Foot Chakras: Put on soles of feet.
- For the Spiritual center, higher self: Spray Frankincense, Lavender, Neroli, or Angelica with a spritzer around top of head.

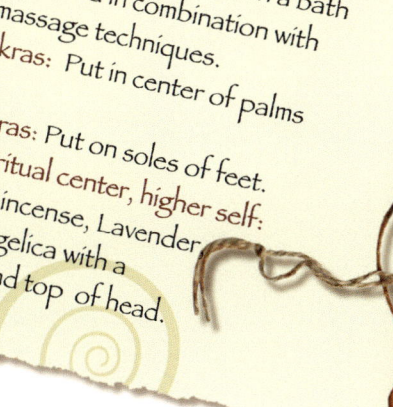

Essential Oils: Nature's Fragrant Garden

Aromas are pure fragrances for healing body, mind and spirit. You can use the aromas in the form of incense, flower essences, and essential oils, or soaps, candles, and sachets. Aromatherapy is used externally and most are diluted with a base oil or carrier oil. Some of the carrier oils that can be chosen are sesame, coconut, sunflower, canola, mustard, sweet almond, avocado, calendula, carrot, hazelnut, jojoba, olive, peanut and wheat germ.

How to Use Essential Oils

Oils can be applied to chakras, alarm points, and emotional stress points and the point at the base of the neck called the release point. They can also be applied to points on the feet, such as K1, and to many points on the hand. Apply to the hand and rotate clockwise to activate.

Bathing:

Using oils in the bath helps unlock congested pores, eases muscle tension and fatigue, quiets the mind and calms the spirit. After running a warm bath, add eight to ten drops of your chosen oil and relax in the bath for at least ten minutes.
Suggested bath oils: Bergamot, Chamomile, Frankincense, Geranium, Jasmine, Lavender, Mandarin, Neroli, Tangerine, Rose, Ylang Ylang. Add vegetable or olive oil for dry skin.

Bath Therapy: Put seven drops from a flower essence or essential oil bottle in the bath water. For best results soak for 30 minutes. Water is a conductor for electrical force. It activates the aura, cleanses the energy fields and releases karmic patterns.

Vaporization/Inhalation:

Inhale the essential oil by putting six to seven drops onto a tissue or cotton ball; take deep breaths for maximum benefit.

Massage:

Choose specific oils to suit the condition and temperament for the massage. Add ten to twelve drops to one ounce of massage oil. **Inhaled as a vapor:** Use two to three drops. Put hot water into a bowl, add the oil, cover your head with a towel, lean over bowl and inhale. Breathe in deeply.

Diffusers:
Use candles or electric diffusers. Diffusers should be made of clay or glass.

Humidifiers:
Add one to nine drops to the water.

Room Sprays:
Four or more drops, per one cup of water.

Anointing:

Use Myrrh, Frankincense, Jasmine, Rose or Lavender on the Third Eye along with stating your affirmation or intention out loud. For protection use Rosemary, Juniper and Vetiver. Put on Solar Plexus and move the energy with a counter-clockwise motion. It is wonderful to use specific oils on the chakras, or on any area of the body that needs attention.

The Bach Flowers for The Chakras

ROOT: Sweet Chestnut – *Trusting yourself*

NAVEL: Wild Rose – *Taking part in life joyfully & fully*

SOLAR PLEXUS: Larch – *Self-awareness*

HEART: Heather – *Unconditional love*

THROAT: Wild Oat – *Communicating from your deepest soul*

THIRD EYE: White chestnut – *Aid to meditation*

CROWN: Olive – *Trusting in cosmic harmony*

Once all other chakras are in balance, the Crown Chakra is also balanced.

Symptoms: How to use Essential Oils

Aches & pains
Massage & Bathing: Lavender, Myrrh, Cinnamon
Inhalation: Basil, Sandalwood

Antibacterial
Massage & Bathing: Jasmine, Sandalwood, Myrrh
Inhalation: Gardenia

Congestion
Inhalation: Eucalyptus, Sage, Basil, Mint

Depression
Massage & Bathing: Lime, Basil, Jasmine, Thyme
Inhalation: Rosemary, Bergamot, Orange, Patchouli, Saffron, Ylang Ylang, Sandalwood

Digestion
Inhalation: Cardamom, Cloves, Marjoram, Lavender

Fatigue
Massage & Bathing: Basil, Cloves, Marjoram
Inhalation: Lavender

Gynecological
Massage & Bathing: Rose, Lemon, Rosemary
Inhalation: Geranium

Essential Oil Recipes
20 to 60 drops base oil per 100ml.
5 to 15 drops per 25ml.
2 to 3 drops per teaspoon.
25ml (12-13 drops per 1 fluid ounce base oil).

Infections
Massage & Bathing: Eucalyptus, Cedar

Immune functions
Massage & Bathing: Myrrh, Frankincense, Rose
Inhalation: Lotus

Insomnia
Massage & Bathing: Marjoram, Lavender, Ylang
Inhalation: Chamomile, Sandalwood

Stress, Tension
Massage & Bathing: Rose, Lavender, Sandalwood
Inhalation: Neroli, Frankincense, Geranium, Clary Sage, Basil, Lotus, Lily

Essential Oils for:

Over-thinking & Worry: Sandalwood, Lemon, Frankincense, Myrrh

Depression & Fear Nervous: Tension: Chamomile, Orange, Bergamot

Disempowerment & Indecision: Ginger, Juniper

Clarity of Mind: Rosemary

Anger & Frustration: Orange, Bergamot, Grapefruit, Peppermint, Chamomile, Yarrow, Lavender, Oil of Rose

Impatience & Intolerance: Bergamot, Lavender, Peppermint

Mental Fatigue: Rosemary, Tea Tree, Laurel

Tension & Agitation: Chamomile, Sweet Orange, Bergamot

Relaxation & Rejuvenation: Frankincense, Lemon, Peppermint

Anxiety & Apprehension: Basil, Bergamot, Clary Sage, Frankincense, Geranium, Grapefruit, Jasmine, Juniper, Lavender, Neroli, Orange, Patchouli, Rose, Sandalwood, Vanilla, Verbena, Vertiver, Ylang Ylang, Thyme

Bitterness: Chamomile, Bergamot

Nerves: Angelica, Basil, Bergamot, Camphor, Cypress, Jasmine, Lavender, Melissa, Neroli, Patchouli, Chamomile, Rose, Rosewood, Sandalwood, Tangerine, Vertiver, Ylang Ylang

Lack of Confidence & Self-Esteem: Rosemary, Jasmine, Rose

Low Morale: Thyme, Pine, Cedarwood

Lack of Self-worth: Rose, Jasmine

Anxiety & Depression: Lavender, Rose

Sudden Fear: Geranium, Vertiver, Rose

Calming: Jasmine, Ylang Ylang

Vulnerability: Pine, Thyme

Resistance to Change: Cypress, Juniper

Chronic Indecisiveness: Clary Sage, Bergamot, Orange

Frustration & Negativity: Bergamot, Orange, Neroli

Lonely & Forlorn: Marjoram, Rosemary, Myrrh

Over-attachment: Frankincense, Myrrh

Joylessness: Jasmine, Ylang Ylang, Orange

Abandonment: Rose, Neroli, Ginger

Depression: Basil, Bergamot, Camphor, Chamomile, Clary Sage, Geranium, Grapefruit, Jasmine, Lavender, Neroli, Patchouli, Rose, Sandalwood, Ylang Ylang

Nervous Tension: Chamomile, Orange, Bergamot, Lavender

Psychic cleanser: Rosemary

Spiritual protection: Rosewood, Sandalwood

The Healing Power of Crystals & Gemstones

Amber

Azurite

Amethyst

Alexandrite

Diamond

Emerald

Garnet

Hematite

Crystals and gemstones have been used for thousands of years for correcting disorders in the physical body and energy fields. In the past, many valuable stones were crushed and reduced to ashes to produce medicines which were ingested orally. Gems may be kept in water, so that the water absorbs their vibration, and are then used as liquid remedies. The healing energy of gems is the energy of white light with specific healing properties. Crystals bring more beauty and light and change the energy of an area. Light reflected off a crystal brings healing and greater harmony. Crystals bring messages of great wisdom as well as energy that heals and transforms.

They have the power to receive, contain, project, emanate and reflect vibrations. Through using crystals it is possible to awaken one's dormant energies and to remove energy blocks. They also help align the energy fields with the greater universal energy fields. Through this alignment our energy fields are raised to a much higher level and we then develop intuition and a deep connection with the source of life. Crystals are mirrors of our soul and can be powerful tools on our transformation path, reflecting our true nature and our soul's gifts. Crystals, the most highly evolved in the mineral kingdom, are symbols of radiant white light energy. All crystals are expressions of light and energy and each has their own rate of vibration.

Agate

Aquamarine

Aventurine

Carnelion

Chalcedony

Jade

Red Jasper

Kunzinite

Heart Kunzinite

Lapis Lazuli

How Crystals are used:
- As remedies
- Worn as a talisman
- For pendulums
- For laying on of stones
- For meditation
- Can be held or worn to absorb properties
- Can be placed in visual range to aid in focusing
- For aura cleansing and balancing
- In jewelry as an aid in maintaining mental clarity, improving concentration and emotional stability.
- Used to clear away emotional debris and to enhance healing abilities.

Care and Cleaning
Place crystals where they can reflect their light and radiate their beauty. Cleanse new stones by soaking in sea salt water for at least three hours.

Recharging
Keep in a well-lighted room.

How to make Crystal Remedies
Place stones or crystals in pure leaded glass; fill with distilled water. Place in the morning sun for about three hours. The water will be infused with the vibration of the crystal as well as the color of the stone. Put in dropper bottles and test regarding the amount to take, or use approximately 10 drops several times a day. Work with the healing affirmations the stones represent. *See list of suggested affirmations along with meanings of stones.*

Suggested Stones for Remedies
Clear quartz, tourmaline, rose, adventurine and amethyst. Stones can also be used with creams or massage oil to enhance the effect of the massage. Green stones produce a healing affect, red and orange stones a revitalization affect, pink enhances love and heart opening, blue is calming and violet intensifies the connection with higher consciousness.

Programming Crystals
Thoughts, wishes and blessings can be programmed into crystals. Simply direct the affirmation or thought into a clear quartz crystal and the crystal will carry the message for you. Crystals will carry out whatever healing intention you might have.

Malachite

Moonstone

Gems & Balancing the Seven Primary Chakras

The seven chakras or centers of vital energy receive and transmit energy in the form of color. Their correct functioning depends on both psychological and health. Gemstone therapy has a direct action on balancing these subtle energy centers.

The Crown Chakra rules the pineal gland, brain and right eye, and is balanced by Emerald, Amethyst, Fire Agate, Labradorite or Malachite and especially Diamond.

The Third Eye Chakra rules the pituitary gland, left eye, ears, nose and nervous system and is balanced by Topaz, Amethyst, Carnelian, Emerald, Labradorite, Malachite, and Sapphire.

The Throat Chakra rules the thyroid gland, bronchial and vocal organs, lungs, alimentary canal, and comes into balance through the Diamond, Amber, Aquamarine, Citrine, Emerald, Lapis Lazuli, Topaz or Turquoise.

The Heart Chakra rules the thymus gland, heart, blood, vagus nerve, and circulatory system and is balanced by Sapphire, Bloodstone and Topaz.

The Solar Plexus Chakra rules the pancreas gland, stomach, liver, nervous system, and gall bladder and comes into balance with Ruby, Amber, Aquamarine, Citrine, Emerald, Moonstone, Pearl and Turquoise.

The Navel Chakra rules the reproductive system and comes into balance by the use of Pearl, Amber, Amethyst, Aquamarine, Carnelian, Coral, Fire Agate, Garnet, and Labradorite.

The Root Chakra rules the adrenals, spinal column, and kidneys and comes into balance through Coral, Garnet, and Turquoise.

To balance the Chakras with the use of crystals or gems, first detect the center that needs balancing (see energy diagnosis page 39) then, when the person is laying down in a relaxed state, apply the stones to the center. (see chakra chart on page 38). Test for length of time. Music and quiet environment are important.

Healing with Gemstones

1. **Root Chakra** – Agate, hematite, blood jasper, garnet, ruby, bloodstone, smoky quartz, onyx, tiger eye.

2. **Navel Chakra** – Carnelian, moonstone, citrine, topaz, coral, tourmaline.

3. **Solar Plexus Chakra** – Citrine, turquoise, lapis, amber, tiger eye, topaz, aventurine, quartz.

4. **Heart Chakra** – Rose Quartz, tourmaline, kunzite, emerald, jade, watermelon tourmaline, azurite, aventurine, quartz, malachite, moonstone.

5. **Throat Chakra** – Aquamarine, turquoise, chalcedony, lapis lazuli, agate, celestite, sodalite, sapphire.

6. **Third Eye Chakra** – Lapis, blue sapphire, sodalite, quartz, opal.

7. **Crown Chakra** – Amethyst, clear quartz, diamond, crystal, topaz, alexanderite, sapphire, selenite.

Opal

Onyx

Quartz

Ruby

Rose Quartz

Selenite

Sodalite

Sapphire

Tourmaline

Tourmaline Watermelon

Topaz

Tiger's Eye

Turquoise

Daily Chakra Balancing Exercises

Chakra Clearing Exercise

1. Sit in a comfortable, easy pose or lotus pose. Root down through your tailbone and elongate your spine. Lift the crown of your head to the ceiling and allow your shoulders to lower away from your ears.

2. Interlace your hands into the Venus Mudra (lock), also known as the Mudra of Love. (Shown to the right)

3. Lift your hands and elbows to your eyebrows, (the Third Eye Chakra). Keep your elbows in line with your hands and inhale fully.

4. Forcefully exhale as you push your hands and arms down until you reach your Navel Chakra (located three finger widths beneath your belly button). Draw your stomach in-and-up at the end of your exhale. Lift your hands on the inhale and repeat this sequence 20-30 times vigorously. Let the inhale become automatic while the exhale stays powerful and forceful. Your eyes may be open or closed during the exercise.

5. Release the Venus Mudra. Close your eyes and with your palms facing your forehead, bring your hands toward the Third Eye Chakra. Return to full yoga breathing; inhale 3 seconds, exhale 3 seconds, until your breath returns to normal.

6. Move your hands from your Third Eye Chakra up to your Crown Chakra. Circle your hands down to the floor and bring your hands up to each chakra; starting at the Root and ending at the Crown. Visualize a white light rejuvenating each chakra center. Repeat these circles 3 times. Continue full yoga breathing.

Chakra Integration – Mother Earth & Father Sky

1. Begin by deeply inhaling and exhaling. Take a moment to focus your energy on your Crown Chakra.

2. Breathe in the energy from above your Crown Chakra and descend the breath down through the chakras, taking a full inhale and exhale at each chakra. Visualize the colors of each chakra as breath through them, and bathe them in a radiant healing light.

   - Crown - White or violet
   - Third Eye - Indigo
   - Throat - Blue
   - Heart - Green
   - Solar Plexus - Yellow
   - Navel - Orange
   - Root - Red

3. Now, with a deep inhalation, bring your arms out to your side.

4. Exhale and bring your hands together in front of your chest in prayer position.

5. Inhale once more and separate your arms away from each other, stretching one high above your head with your hands flat above the sky as if you were pushing the sky open – while the other arm reaches down flat as if you were pushing something downward toward Mother Earth. Gaze up at the heavens, (Father Sky). Stay in this position for 3 deep breaths.

6. Now, exhale as you return your hands to the prayer position, in front of your heart.

7. Repeat. This time switch your arms so the opposite arm rises to the sky while the other one pushes toward the earth.

8. Repeat up to 3 times for maximum benefit.

"The mind turned inward is the Self; turned outward, it becomes the Ego and all the world.
– Sri Ramana Maharshi

Daily Chakra Balancing Exercises

Chakra Illuminating Exercise: Yogi Spinal Twist

This exercise is very beneficial at balancing the right and left hemispheres of the brain, strengthening the lower back, rejuvenating the digestive system and increasing flexibility in the hips and torso. Yogi Spinal Twists also aim to stimulate or awaken Kundalini Shakti and encourage her to rise through the Sushumna channel and illuminate the chakras.

1. Sit in a comfortable, easy pose or lotus pose. Root down through your tailbone and elongate your spine. Lift the crown of your head to the ceiling and allow your shoulders to lower away from your ears.

2. Bring your hands to rest on your shoulders with the fingers on front and the thumbs on the back of the shoulders. Keep your elbows lifted in line with the shoulders. Make sure your shoulders stay lowered away from your ears during the exercise. Engage your abdominal muscles by drawing your belly button in and up toward your spine.

3. Inhale through your nose as you twist to the left, allow your gaze to follow your twist. Exhale through your nose as you twist to the right.

4. Repeat the twisting and allow this motion to gain speed. Close your eyes. Visualize the energy at the Root Chakra traveling up the spine, touching all the chakras and rising out of the Crown Chakra.

5. Perform this exercise for a minute. Slowly return to center and allow the hands to return to your knees, palms facing up. Focus on the Third Eye Chakra, visualize an indigo light between the eyebrows.

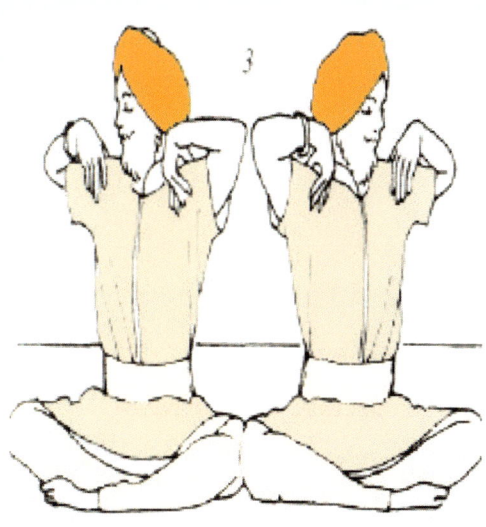

Balancing Your Chakras
Through Yoga!

- ROOT
- NAVEL
- SOLAR PLEXUS
- HEART
- THROAT
- THIRD EYE
- CROWN

The Sun Salutation also Balances all the Chakras

Daily Chakra Balancing Exercises

Protection Ceremonies

Breathe deeply and center yourself in your heart. On the inhalation, breath in a beautiful golden light and surround yourself with this sphere of light as you exhale.

Affirm: "I am strong, protected and shielded by divine light."

Shielding Techniques – Use of Energy Sheilds

Visualize a golden disk, full of light and protection, and mentally place it over the chakras that need protection, especially the Solar Plexus Chakra.

Chakra Balancing Mudras

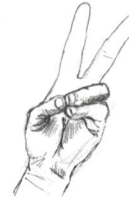

Prana Mudra – Vital Force. Awakens the Root, Navel and Solar Plexus Chakras. Improves energy, circulation, eyesight and general health. Increases vital force. Join the tips of your little finger, ring finger and thumb. Concentrate on your breathing.

Padma Mudra – Blossoming Lotus. Awakens the Heart Chakra. Elevates heart energy, integrates body and mind. Place hands together in front of your Heart Chakra. Keep your thumbs and little fingers together, blossom the other fingers outward and create a cup shape between your palms.

Jnana Mudra – Attaining Wisdom. Awakens the Throat, Third Eye and Crown Chakras. Aids in concentration, meditation, memory and brain power. Brings a sense of peace to all aspects of the body and mind and balances the three higher chakras. Touch the tip of the thumb with the tip of the index finger. Use for anytime relaxation is needed. Fingers are pointing upward, but not fully extended.

Chakra Balancing Mantra

BIJA MANTRA – OM – AUM

"Uttering the monosyllable "Om" the eternal world of Brahman, One who departs leaving the body (at death), he attains the superior goal."
Bhagavad Gita, 8.13

The "AUM" sound is sometimes called "the 4-syllable Veda." When correctly pronounced, "AUM" is said to have four sounds: "A" emerges from the throat, originating in the region of the navel. "U" rolls over the tongue, and "M" ends on the lips. The last sound is silence.

Sit in a comfortable easy pose and chant "OM" three times. Repeat whenever you need to remember you connection with your Source.

Jewels offers guidance on how to tap the magnificent being that you are. During this time of evolutionary awakening we are guided to take a step into our divine potential. *Jewels* invites you to take this step and enter the temple of your inner light, where you are simply asked to let go of all that is prohibiting you from experiencing your radiant being.

Arielle is a certified yoga teacher and movement instructor. She offers accessible methods for everyday people to align and cleanse their energy body and awaken their chakras. Through pranyama, mudras, mantras, simple energy exercises and yoga, she aims to get students in a state of harmony in their body, mind, and spirit so they are able to truly renew and awaken.

Jewels of Light is a series of books, audio, video, trainings, events, sacred art and services. For more information on all the Chakras; order the L.E.A.P. Manual (Life Essence Awakening Process™) or Enroll in our online Correspondence Courses at www.AwakeningYourChakras.com.

Own The Jewels of Light Series & Products

Book 1: Well Being - Body, Mind & Spirit
Book 2: The Path of Return
Book 3: Trust In Yourself
Book 4: Living Meditations

Awakening Your Chakras
(Hard & Soft cover - with full color illustrations)

Additional Books:
• *Life Essence Awakening Manual*

Products
• *Individual Chakra Posters* • *Kundalini Chakra Poster*
Reference Charts • *Jewels Happiness Poster*
• *Chakra Blessing Oracle Deck* • *Chakra Jeweled Greeting Cards*
• *Coordinated Bookmarks* • *Chakra Note Cards* • *Gemstones* • *Essential Oils*
• *Chakra Pendulums & Jewelry* • *Chakra Spa Line*

Plus . . .

- *Books*
- *Videos*
- *eBooks*
- *Charts & Posters*
- *Training & Education*
- *Seminar Information*
- *Audio Books*
- *Calendar of Events*
- *Free Downloads*
- *& More!*

Our Ascension Yoga Apparel can be purchased at:
www.AscensionYogaApparel.com

For more information please visit:
www.JewelsofLight.com • www.AwakeningYourChakras.com
Or call toll free: 1.855.50 JEWEL (505.3935)

CPSIA information can be obtained
at www.ICGtesting.com
Printed in the USA
LVIC06n2257031216
515466LV00006B/13